...ER PATILLA

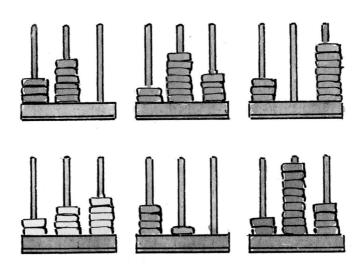

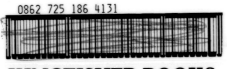

KINGFISHER BOOKS

Kingfisher Books, Grisewood & Dempsey Ltd,
Elsley House, 24–30 Great Titchfield Street,
London W1P 7AD

First published in 1990 by Kingfisher Books
Text Copyright © Peter Patilla 1990
Illustrations © Grisewood and Dempsey Ltd 1990

BRITISH LIBRARY CATALOGUING IN PUBLICATION DATA
Patilla, Peter
Good subtracting.
1. Arithmetic. Subtraction
I. Title   II. McKenna, Terry   III. Series
513'.2

ISBN 0-86272-518-6

Editor: John Grisewood

Illustrations: Terry McKenna

Design: Robert Wheeler Design Associates

Phototypeset by Southern Positives and Negatives, (SPAN),
Lingfield, Surrey

Printed in Spain

513·2

0862 725 186 4131

Contents

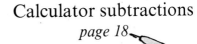

Taking away

There are many different kinds of subtraction. One sort of subtraction is called 'taking away', when what you started with becomes smaller.

Try these take away activities.

Abacus numbers

Here are some numbers on an abacus.

Take away 12 from each abacus number and draw the answers on your own abaci.

Halving

Take away half of each HTU (hundred, ten, unit) number and draw what is left.

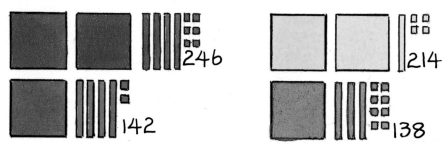

246

214

142

138

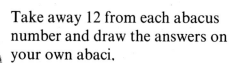

4

Nim

Nim is a game which involves taking away. It needs two players and 20 small objects to start with.

Take turns to remove 1, 2, 3 or 4 of the objects.
The player who takes the last object or objects wins.

Play several games.
Can you find a way of winning?

Try changing the number of objects you start with.

Smaller measures

Sometimes we take away from lengths and quantities.

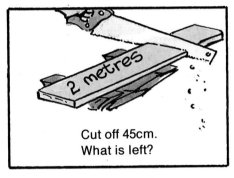

Cut off 45cm.
What is left?

Drink 500ml.
What is left?

Eat 125g.
What is left?

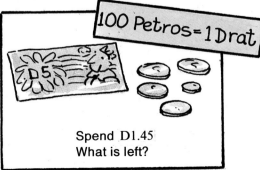

100 Petros = 1 Drat

Spend D1.45
What is left?

Difference

There is a type of subtraction called 'difference'. Nothing is actually taken away when finding the difference between two numbers. It is comparing two numbers finding how many more, or less, one number is than the other.

> The difference between 6 and 10 is 4.
> The difference between 5m and 2m is 3m.

Try these difference activities.

Pairs
Find the difference between each pair of coins.

100 Petros (P) = 1 Drat (D)

Card game

Use a pack of cards without the picture cards.
Three cards are dealt to each player.
The rest of the cards are placed face down.
Players take a card from the pack in turn.
When a difference of 3 can be made that pair of cards is placed face down.
Another turn can be had whenever a pair is made.
The winner is the player who gets rid of all their cards first or who has the smallest total in their hand at the end.
Play the game again but change the difference.

Digit cards

Make digit cards 1 to 9.
Find a home for each card.
The stars show the difference between adjacent numbers.

Difference challenge

You are only allowed to use these four digits.
How many different answers can be made by finding differences?

$6 - 3 = 3$ $8 - 2 = 6$ $23 - 6 = 17$

Domino difference

These domino totals have a difference of 4.

Can you draw other domino pairs which have a difference of 4?

Complementary addition

Another type of subtraction is called 'complementary addition'. This is often the method used by shopkeepers when counting out your change. Complementary addition is adding on from one number to another.

All change

In the country of Dratonia the currency is as follows:
100 petros = 1 Drat.
There are denominations of D1, 50p, 20p, 10p, 5p, and 1p.
The shopkeeper uses the fewest number of coins she can when giving change. Which coins will she give as change when 5 Drat is offered as payment?

Number chains

Two numbers can be subtracted using complementary addition and number chains.

94 take away 37.

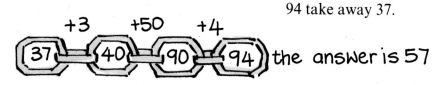

the answer is 57

Try these chains yourself.
Different chains are possible between each pair of numbers.

Equations

Use complementary addition skills to find the missing numbers in these equations.

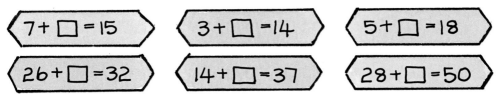

7 + ☐ = 15   3 + ☐ = 14   5 + ☐ = 18

26 + ☐ = 32   14 + ☐ = 37   28 + ☐ = 50

Time check

How many minutes are there between the times shown on each pair of watches?

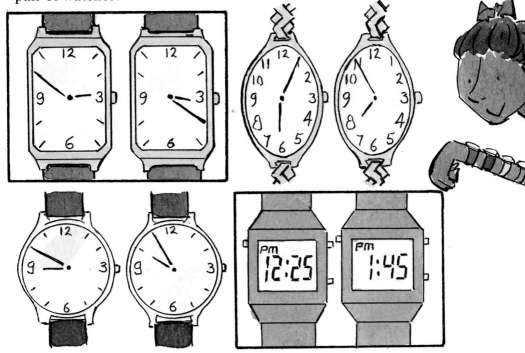

pm 12:25   pm 1:45

Round up

What must be added to each of these numbers to round them up to the next 100?

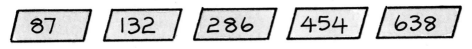

87   132   286   454   638

9

Subtraction games

Four in a line

A game for two players.
A calculator can be used.
Players take turns to choose two
star numbers and find the
difference between them.
If the difference is on the grid
cover it with a small counter
(pieces of card will do).
The first player to get four
counters in a straight line,
horizontally, vertically or
diagonally wins.

19	28	41	10	31	11
32	61	50	63	25	55
47	53	22	44	40	34
62	15	66	23	38	21
·60	22	33	14	29	17
54	10	12	74	30	16

27 63 78 25 17 77 60 50 48 80 16 46 70 30 91

Calculator game

Start with 100 on the display.
Take turns to subtract any
number which is less than 10.
Who will be the player to reach
zero?

Dice game

Players draw empty boxes like this.

Roll a dice.
Each player writes the number rolled in any one of the boxes.
(Do not let the other players see where you put the numbers.)
Roll the dice again and put the number in another box.
Keep doing this until all six boxes are full.
Each player subtracts their two numbers.
The player with the answer nearest to 150 wins.

Nine lives game

Each player begins with nine lives.

Copy the grid.
Join two dots with a straight line.
Try to complete squares.
If you complete a square which
has − 1 inside it then you lose
one of your lives.
The winner is the player with
most lives left at the end of the
game.

Subtracting large numbers

How good are you at subtracting two and three digit numbers? Try your skills out on these activities.

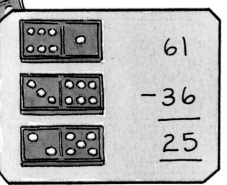

$$61$$
$$-36$$
$$\overline{25}$$

Domino problem

Here is a subtraction problem made from three dominoes. Make some different domino subtractions and draw the answers.

Digit switch

You can use a calculator to help you explore this number pattern activity.

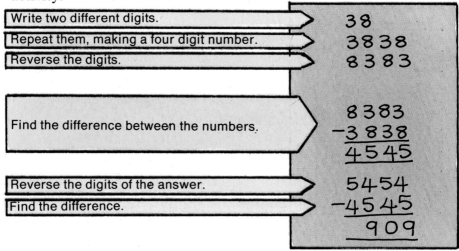

Write two different digits.		38
Repeat them, making a four digit number.		3838
Reverse the digits.		8383

Find the difference between the numbers.

$$8383$$
$$-3838$$
$$\overline{4545}$$

| Reverse the digits of the answer. | | 5454 |
| Find the difference. | | -4545 |

$$\overline{909}$$

Keep doing this until you have an answer with only three digits.

Repeat with a different pair of starting digits.
Can you guess what the answers will be each time?

Darts scores

Subtraction skills are needed when playing darts.
Find each darts total.
Subtract the total from the player's score.

Claire 301

CLEVER
CLAIRE

Alan 301

ARROWS
ALAN

Consecutives

Numbers which come after each other are called 'consecutive'.

23 and 24 are consecutive. 45 and 46 are also consecutive.

Can you find the missing consecutive numbers in these equations?

$$157 - \square - \triangle = 100 \qquad 213 - \square - \triangle = 100$$

$$171 - \square - \triangle = 100 \qquad 187 - \square - \triangle = 100$$

$$239 - \square - \triangle = 100$$

Subtraction puzzles

Try and solve these puzzles using all your skills of subtraction.

Word teaser

In this problem each letter
stands for a number.
The letter E = 4 and S = 6
Can you find what the other
letters stand for?

Now try this problem.
The letter H = 9 and E = 4

(There may be more
than one answer)

Code wheel

Find the answers to the subtractions.
Use the wheel code to find the letters.
Rearrange the letters to discover the names of some cities.

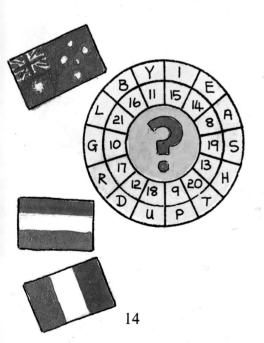

Subtract 9 from each number
22   26   29   23   18
(*A city in Australia*)

Subtract 7 from each number
21   15   25   17   20
(*A city in the Netherlands*)

Subtract 8 from each number
27   17   25   16   23
(*A city in France*)

Bubble puzzle

Take:
A number from the first bubble.
A sign from the second bubble.
A number from the third bubble.
The correct answer from
the fourth bubble.
Do this till the bubbles are empty.

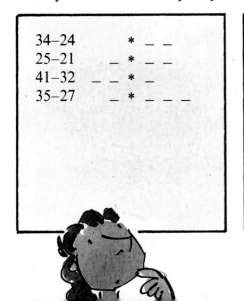

Mystery names

Look at the subtraction problems.
Write the answers in words.
Line up the words as shown.
Can you discover the mystery names?

34–24	* _ _
25–21	_ * _ _
41–32	_ _ * _
35–27	_ * _ _ _

33–26	* _ _ _ _
37–29	_ _ _ _ *
31–28	_ _ _ * _
32–25	_ _ * _ _
27–18	_ _ _ *
38–29	_ _ * _

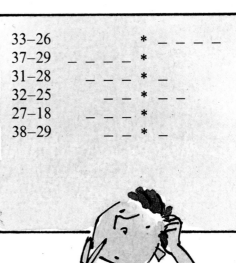

Investigating subtractions

When trying some of these investigations remember that there may be lots of different answers to the problems. Don't stop once you have found one possible answer. Do explore and find other different solutions.

Number cards

Make some small cards numbered 1–9.

Use the cards to make a set of subtraction problems.

Here is a set of two problems which uses six of the cards.

The cards 3 4 6 have not been used.

How many different sets of subtraction problems can you make using the cards.?

Can you make a set of three problems which uses all the cards.?

Making answers

Use these digits.

Put them into pairs with a subtraction sign between them.

Can you make answers of:

| 27 | 33 | 22 |

How many different answers can you make using other pairs?

Forbidden keys

The challenge is to find ways of doing these subtraction problems
on a calculator without touching the 2 key.

$$\begin{array}{r} 72 \\ 38 \\ \hline \end{array}$$
$$\begin{array}{r} 91 \\ 26 \\ \hline \end{array}$$

$$\begin{array}{r} 120 \\ -32 \\ \hline \end{array}$$
$$\begin{array}{r} 242 \\ 29 \\ \hline \end{array}$$

Start and finish

Start with the number 20.
Finish with the number 3.
You can only subtract.
How many ways can you find?

$$20 - 17 = 3$$

$$20 - 14 - 3 = 3$$

$$20 - 15 - 2 = 3$$

4 Calculator subtractions

A calculator is a useful tool in helping you find answers to subtraction problems. It can also be used to help you explore and discover new things about numbers.

Lift off

You can only touch these keys

[2] [5] [6] [−] [=]

Each key can be touched as often as you wish.
They can be touched in any order.
Not all of them have to be touched.

Here is one way of making 10.   [2] [5] [−] [5] [−] [5] [−] [5]

Make each of these answers for lift off...

9 8 7 6 5 4 3 2 1 ZERO

Time warp

Try going backwards in time.

What was happening...

a million seconds ago
a million hours ago
a million days ago
a million weeks ago

Were you alive? Was there T.V.?
How did people travel?

Super change

Change **278** to **19**

Touch the fewest number of keys possible.
How many keys did you touch?

Try these super changes.

764 to **28**   **301** to **85**   **724** to **56**

Subtraction words

Find the answer to 9034 − 1929.

Turn your calculator upside down and you will see something
that seeds grow in.

Make up some subtraction problems which will show these words
when the calculator is turned upside down.

BIBLE	SLOS	SOLE
hILL	LOOSE	OBOE

Find some calculator words of your own and write subtraction
problems which make them.

Subtraction problems

There are all sorts of different subtraction problems. Some are simple and straightforward while others are tricky and make you think.

Try these different sorts of problems.

Brackets first

Bracket problem

When brackets are in a problem you work out the bracket part first.

$17 - (9 - 5) =$

Work out $9 - 5$ first.
The answer to the problem is 13.

$(17 - 9) - 5 =$

Work out $17 - 9$ first.
The answer to the problem is 3.

In these problems the brackets have been missed out.
Can you find where to put them to make each answer 13?

$18 - 3 - 2$	$15 - 4 - 2$	$24 - 3 + 8$
$9 + 11 - 7$	$18 - 8 - 5 - 2$	$16 - 2 - 9 - 8$

Mental Problems

Take away a quarter from one. Subtract half from three quarters. Find the difference between a quarter and three quarters

Word problems

If 100 petros equals 1 Drat, what change will be received if I spend 345 petros and offer five Drats in payment?

How many minutes are there between 3.40pm and 4.25pm?

Digit card problem
Each of the digit cards
has a home.
Can you find where it is?

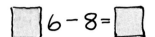 6 – 8 = ☐

4 ☐
–1 ☐
‾‾‾‾
2 4

6 ☐
–3 ☐
‾‾‾‾
☐ 7

☐ 4
– ☐
‾‾‾‾
☐ 7

Abacus problems
Look at the numbers shown on these abacuses

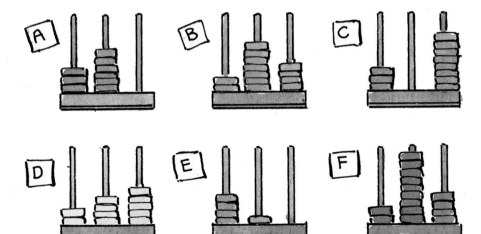

Which pairs of abacuses have. . .

the largest difference   an odd difference

a difference of 20   the smallest difference

Missing numbers in subtractions

Some algebra work is concerned with 'missing numbers'. Try and find the missing numbers in the following activities.

Simple equations

Each of the equations has a missing number.
There is only one possible answer for each equation.

$$16 - 9 = \square \qquad 24 - \square = 13 \qquad \square - 5 = 17$$

Open equations

Sometimes equations can have several possible answers.
There are two missing numbers in each of these equations.
Find different pairs of numbers for each equation to make it true.

$$\square - \triangle = 3 \qquad \square - 4 = \triangle \qquad 12 - \square = \triangle$$

Subtraction sequences

Find the missing numbers in these subtraction sequences.

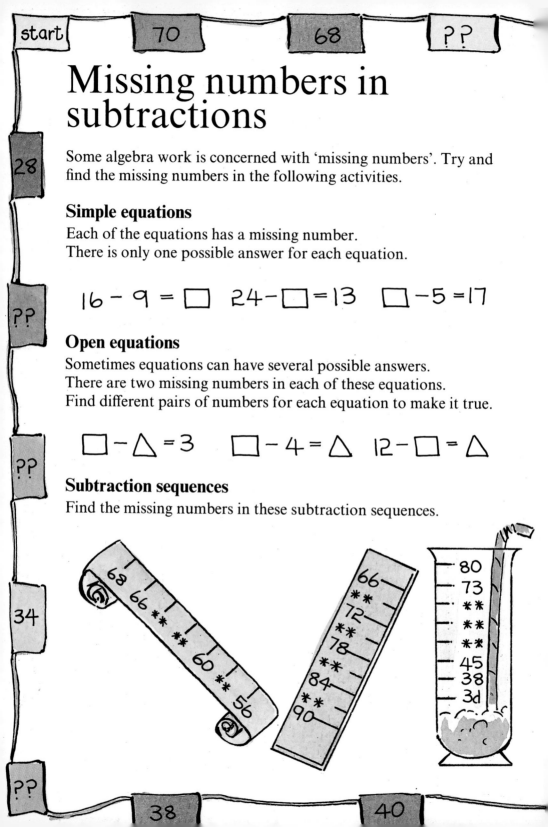

Missing digits

Each star is a missing digit.
Use your subtraction skills to discover each missing digit.

$$
\begin{array}{r} 8* \\ -\,28 \\ \hline *9 \end{array}
\qquad
\begin{array}{r} 50 \\ -\,** \\ \hline 13 \end{array}
\qquad
\begin{array}{r} *2 \\ -\,56 \\ \hline 3* \end{array}
\qquad
\begin{array}{r} 7* \\ -\,*3 \\ \hline 60 \end{array}
\qquad
\begin{array}{r} ** \\ -\,25 \\ \hline 56 \end{array}
$$

Subtraction grids

Here are some subtraction grids with numbers missing.
Find the missing numbers.

−	8	9	10
12	4		
15			
20			

−		9	12
13	6		
			4
24			

−			
	9	8	7
	10	9	8
	11	10	9

Word problems

My difference is 5.
My total is 23.
Which two numbers am I?

Subtract 22 from me
then halve me.
The answer is 14.
What is my number?

Difference walls

Look carefully at this difference wall.
Can you see the number pattern?

Find missing numbers from these walls.

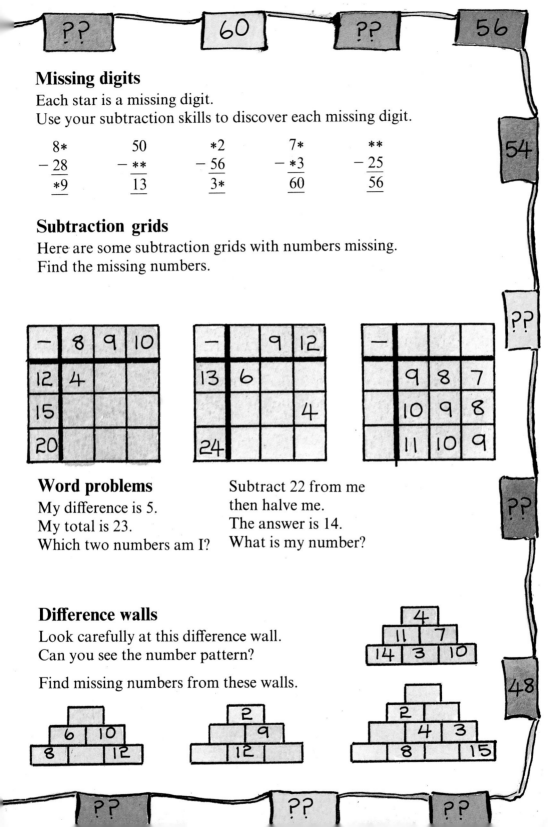

Number patterns and subtraction

Investigating and exploring number patterns is an important part of algebra.
Have fun exploring these number patterns.

Pyramid pattern

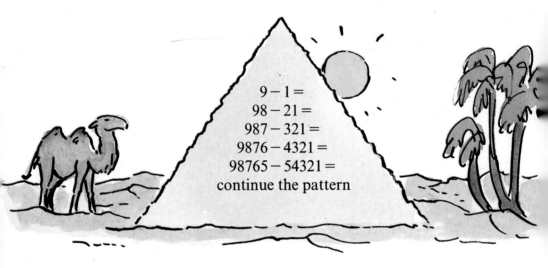

$$9 - 1 =$$
$$98 - 21 =$$
$$987 - 321 =$$
$$9876 - 4321 =$$
$$98765 - 54321 =$$
continue the pattern

Square subtractions

To get a SQUARE NUMBER multiply two identical numbers together.
Here are some square numbers.

$16 = (4 \times 4)$ $36 = (6 \times 6)$ $144 = (12 \times 12)$

Which two square numbers have been subtracted to give these answers?

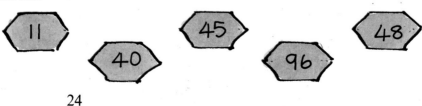

11   45   48
40   96

Reversing digits

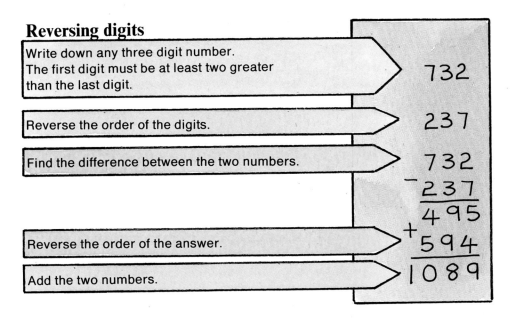

Write down any three digit number. The first digit must be at least two greater than the last digit.	732
Reverse the order of the digits.	237
Find the difference between the two numbers.	732 −237 495
Reverse the order of the answer.	+594
Add the two numbers.	1089

Repeat this with some three digit numbers of your own.
What do you notice?

Odds and evens

Which kind of number do you get if you subtract...

2 odd numbers

2 even numbers

an odd
and an
even
number

25

Subtracting with measures

Temperature drop
What is the temperature shown on these thermometers?

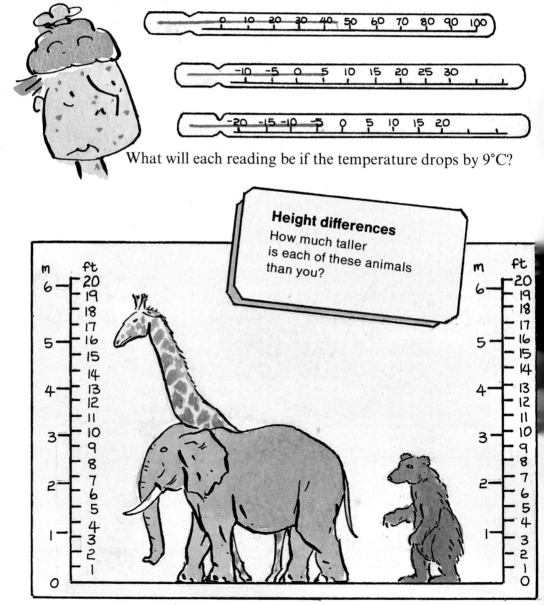

0 10 20 30 40 50 60 70 80 90 100

-10 -5 0 5 10 15 20 25 30

-20 -15 -10 -5 0 5 10 15 20

What will each reading be if the temperature drops by 9°C?

Height differences
How much taller is each of these animals than you?

m   ft
6 — 20
     19
     18
     17
5 — 16
     15
     14
4 — 13
     12
     11
3 — 10
     9
     8
2 — 7
     6
     5
     4
1 — 3
     2
     1
0

m   ft
6 — 20
     19
     18
     17
5 — 16
     15
     14
4 — 13
     12
     11
3 — 10
     9
     8
2 — 7
     6
     5
     4
1 — 3
     2
     1
     0

Time check

Each of these clocks is 20 minutes fast.
What is the correct time for each clock?

Metric

Find the difference
between these
metric measures...

2.50m	3.25m
650g	175g
1.7 litres	2.5 litres
85cl	48cl
146cm	205cm
250ml	135ml

Imperial

In each of these pairs
which is the smaller
measure...

1 inch or 1 centimetre?

1 yard or 1 metre?

1 pound or 1 kilogram?

1 gallon or 1 litre?

27

Subtraction and data handling

Information is presented to us in all sorts of ways...

graphs tables lists charts Pictures maps diagrams

See if you can gather information from these sources.

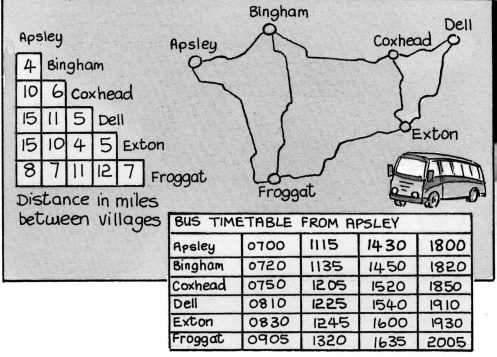

Apsley

4	Bingham
10	6	Coxhead
15	11	5	Dell
15	10	4	5	Exton
8	7	11	12	7	Froggat

Distance in miles
between villages

BUS TIMETABLE FROM APSLEY				
Apsley	0700	1115	1430	1800
Bingham	0720	1135	1450	1820
Coxhead	0750	1205	1520	1850
Dell	0810	1225	1540	1910
Exton	0830	1245	1600	1930
Froggat	0905	1320	1635	2005

● Which is the shortest route from Apsley to Dell?

● What is the difference in mileage going from Bingham to Exton by way of Froggat rather than through Coxhead?

● How many minutes does it take the bus to travel between Dell and Exton?

● How long does it take the bus to travel between Apsley and Coxhead?

Glossary

Complementary addition   Calculating what must be added onto one number to make it the same as another number.

Consecutive numbers   These are numbers which follow on from each other e.g. 10, 11, 12 and 56, 57, 58, 59.

Difference   To find the difference between two numbers subtract them.
e.g. The difference between 20 and 26 is 6.

Digits   The digits are: 0, 1, 2, 3, 4, 5, 6, 7, 8, 9
Some numbers have two digits (35, 78, 95)
Some numbers have three digits (108, 567, 856).

Even numbers   Numbers which can be divided exactly by two.
Here are some even numbers: 2, 6, 18, 74, 90, 142.

Imperial measures   Units used for measuring. The common ones still being used are:
Capacity – Pints (pts) Gallons (gals)
Length – Yards (yds) Feet (ft)
Inches (ins)
Weight – Ounces (oz) Pounds (lb).

Odd numbers   Numbers which cannot be divided by two without leaving a remainder.
Here are some odd numbers: 3, 5, 27, 41, 89, 125.

Square numbers   A square number is obtained by multiplying a number by itself.
36 is a square number because $6 \times 6 = 36$
81 is a square number because $9 \times 9 = 81$.

Sum   To sum a set of numbers means to add them together. The sum of 12, 20 and 34 is 66.

Answers

Page 4
Abacus numbers
022   030   018   009   088
Halving
123   107   71   69

Page 5
Smaller measures
1.55m   (155cm)   500ml   375g   D3.55

Page 6
Pairs
15p   90p   30p   95p

Page 7
Digit cards   *Difference challenge*
7 1 5   There are more than 20
8 3 9   different answers.
4 6 2

Page 8
All change
(10p, 50p, D1)
(2p, 2p, 20p, 50p, D1, D1, D1)
(1p, 2p, 5p, 20p, 20p)
(2p, 2p, 5p, D1, D1)
2p, 20p, D1, D1, D1)

Page 9
Equations
$7+8=15$ $3+11=14$ $5+13=18$
$26+6=32$ $14+23=37$ $28+22=50$

Time check
30min   110min   65min   80min

Round up
13   68   14   46   62

Page 12
Digit switch
The answer will always be the same.

Page 13
Darts score
Claire: 250   Alan: 263

Consecutives
$157-28-29=100$
$213-56-57=100$
$171-35-36=100$
$187-43-44=100$
$239-69-70=100$

Page 14
Word teaser
There are several possible answers e.g.

$$\begin{array}{r} 268 \\ -\ \ 94 \\ \hline 174 \end{array} \qquad \begin{array}{r} 9456 \\ -\ \ 72 \\ \hline 9384 \end{array}$$

Code wheel
Perth, Hague, Paris

Page 15
Bubble puzzle
$10-3=7$ $14-5=9$
$17-9=8$ $12-8=4$ $15-10=5$

Mystery names
Toni   Steven

Page 20
Bracket problem
$(18-3)-2$ $15-(4-2)$ $24-(3+8)$
$9+(11-7)$ $18-(8-5)-2$
$16-2-(9-8)$

Mental problems
three quarters,   one quarter,   half

Word problems
155petros   45 minutes

Page 21
Digit card problem
$16 - 8 = 8$

$$\begin{array}{r} 40 \\ -\ 16 \\ \hline 24 \end{array} \qquad \begin{array}{r} 69 \\ -\ 32 \\ \hline 37 \end{array} \qquad \begin{array}{r} 54 \\ -\ 7 \\ \hline 47 \end{array}$$

Abaci problem
A&D, D and any other one, B&F, C&D

Page 22
Simple equations
$16 - 9 = 7$ $24 - 11 = 13$ $22 - 5 = 17$

Open equations

3, 0	4, 0	0, 12
4, 1	5, 1	1, 11
5, 2	6, 2	2, 10
6, 3 etc	7, 3 etc	3, 9
		etc to
		12, 0

Subtraction sequences

68	66	64	62	60	58	56	
90	87	84	81	78	75	72	69
80	73	66	59	52	45	38	31

Page 23
Missing digits

$$\begin{array}{r} 87 \\ -\ 28 \\ \hline 59 \end{array} \quad \begin{array}{r} 50 \\ -\ 37 \\ \hline 13 \end{array} \quad \begin{array}{r} 92 \\ -\ 56 \\ \hline 36 \end{array} \quad \begin{array}{r} 73 \\ -\ 13 \\ \hline 60 \end{array} \quad \begin{array}{r} 81 \\ -\ 25 \\ \hline 56 \end{array}$$

Subtraction grids

−	8	9	10
12	4	3	2
15	7	6	5
20	12	11	10

−	7	9	12
13	6	4	1
16	9	7	4
24	17	15	12

−	5	6	7
14	9	8	7
15	10	9	8
16	11	10	9

Word problems
14, 9   50

Difference walls

4	2	1
6 10	7 9	2 1
8 2 12	5 12 3	2 4 3
		6 8 12 15

Page 24
Square subtractions
36–25   49–9   81–36   100–4   64–16

Page 25
Reversing digits
The answer will always be 1089

Odds and evens
even, even, odd

Page 26
45°C   5°C   − 4°C
36°C   − 4°C   − 13°C

Page 27
Time check
3.45   9.25   17.55   1.05   9.15   2.30

Metric
0.75m (75cm)   475g
0.8 litres   37cl   59cm   115ml

Imperial
cm   yard   pound   litre

Page 28
Shortest route: Apsley, Bingham, Coxhead, Dell (15 miles); 4 miles; 20min; 50min

Index